By Nader Bolour

The Old...
The New...
The Future!

DLB
Doris Leslie Blau

A Pictorial Journal

Carpets were never just carpets. They were these breathtaking pieces of art that told a story, and as fate would have it, become a part of my life forever. It all started in 1967 as a 12 year old boy, spending my summer days as a child cleaning and admiring them. I was destined to meet Doris Blau, the reigning rug queen for more than 40 years. There was a strong connection between Doris and I the second we met. We shared the same eye and a similar way of conducting business, aesthetics and ethics with a passion. As the owner of DLB, it is with great pleasure to showcase through this catalogue a glimpse at some of the diverse eclectic art forms we have for the floor. We present to you some old, some new and as for the future… we'll let your creativity and mind be the force that drives our future designs.

— Nader Bolour, owner

The Old...

Our collection of antique oriental and European carpets speak of the past histories of diverse cultures and are as exciting today as they were a hundred years ago.

The excitement and sensual qualities that purveyed our dramatic and whimsical examples situate them for placement in contemporary and antique settings, which takes flair and imagination.

To assimilate an oriental antique into a western design demands daring and wit; and to integrate an exotic oriental antique into a familiar setting takes a designer of singular talent and with the lightest but surest of touches. The most superlative schemes are often those where such risks are undertaken boldly, where genres are successfully blended, and contrasting styles are used to accentuate diversity whilst still creating harmony.

It is as always, both my personal commitment and goal to continue bringing a bit of "soul" to each room and every project.

6   BB4025 Meshad 24'9" × 17'7"

BB5220 Tabriz 12'2″ × 10'2″

BB4338 Indian 16'7″ × 10'10″

BB4585 Khorassan 9' × 6'8"

BB4319 Malayer 15' × 10'

BB5065 Heriz 15'2" × 10'8"

12   BB4346 Sultanabad 18'4″ × 11'3″

BB4195 Meshad 11'10″ × 8'3″   13

14   BB4774 Kirman 22'6″ × 13'5″

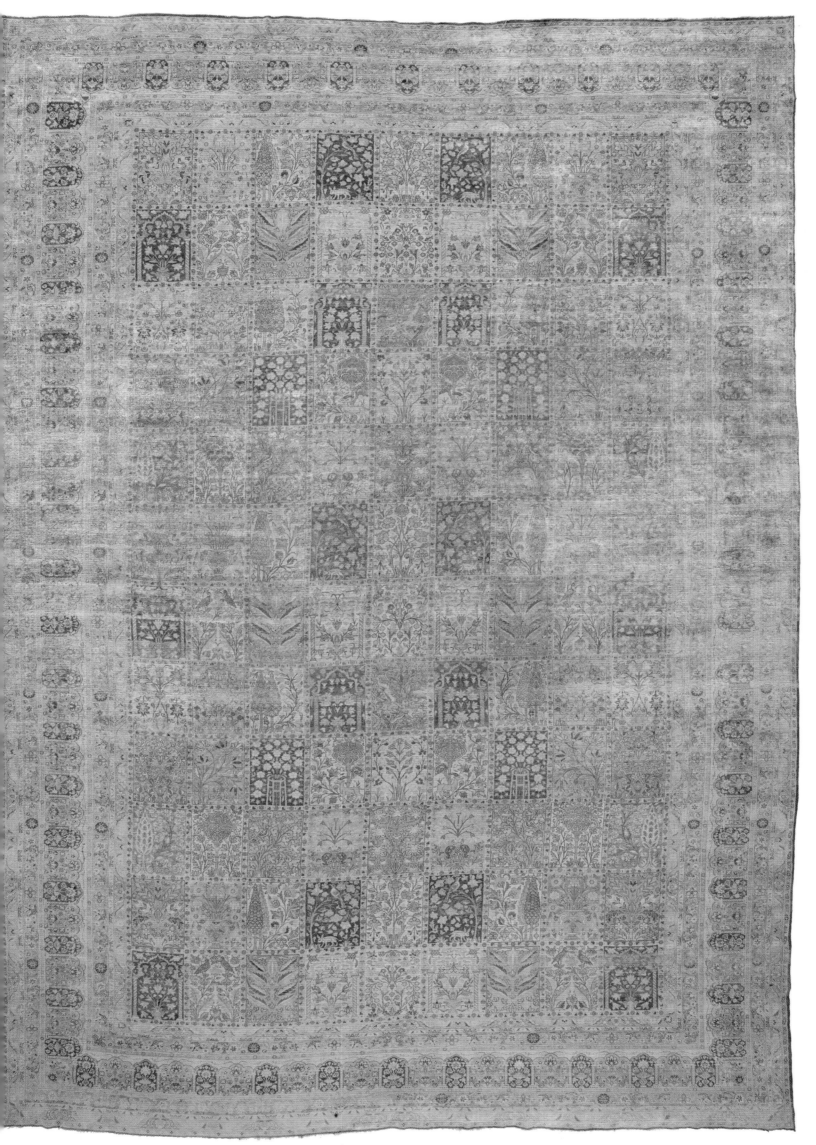

BB3444 Kirman 19'6" × 12'8"

16   BB4859 Tabriz 18'3" × 12'

BB4498 Silk Tabriz Garden Carpet 10'6″ × 7'

18   BB3619 Kirman 19' × 11'10"

BB4280 Meshad 12'3" × 9'9"

20   BB4956 Indian (size adjusted) 17'3" × 12'10"

BB4452 Kashan 15'7″ × 9'10″

22   BB4355 Kirman 17'9" × 12'9"

BB3308 Tabriz 12'9" × 9'3" 23

BB2520 Meshad 17'3″ × 10'

BB4965 Tabriz 10'2″ × 8'2″

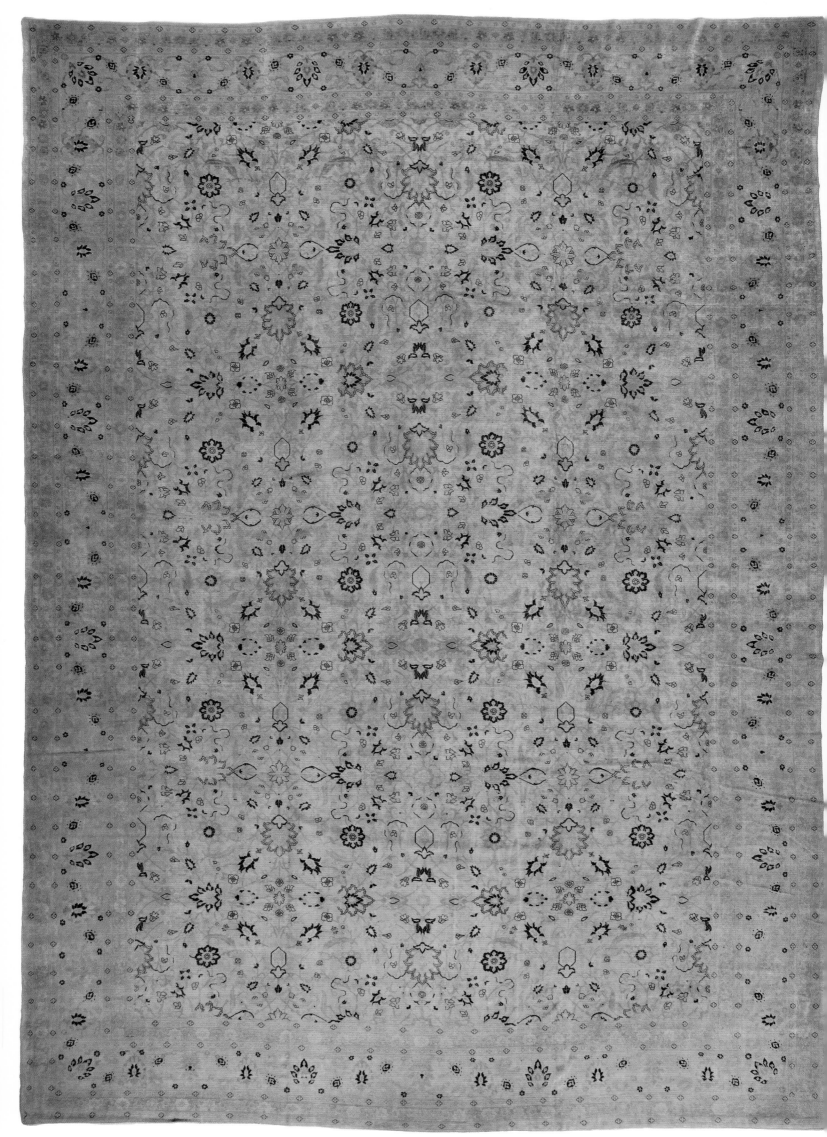

26   BB3843 Tabriz 21'5" × 14'2"

BB3045 Sarouk 11'10" × 9'

28   BB4305 Sultanabad 14'7" × 10'10"

BB3553 Sultanabad 17'2″ × 13'2″

30   BB4246 Sultanabad (size adjusted) 19'10" × 13'10"

BB5163 English Needlework (attributed to Pontremoli) 21'10" × 13'8"   31

32   BB0897 Oushak 15'3" × 11'8"

BB2508 Oushak 14'6" × 9'2"

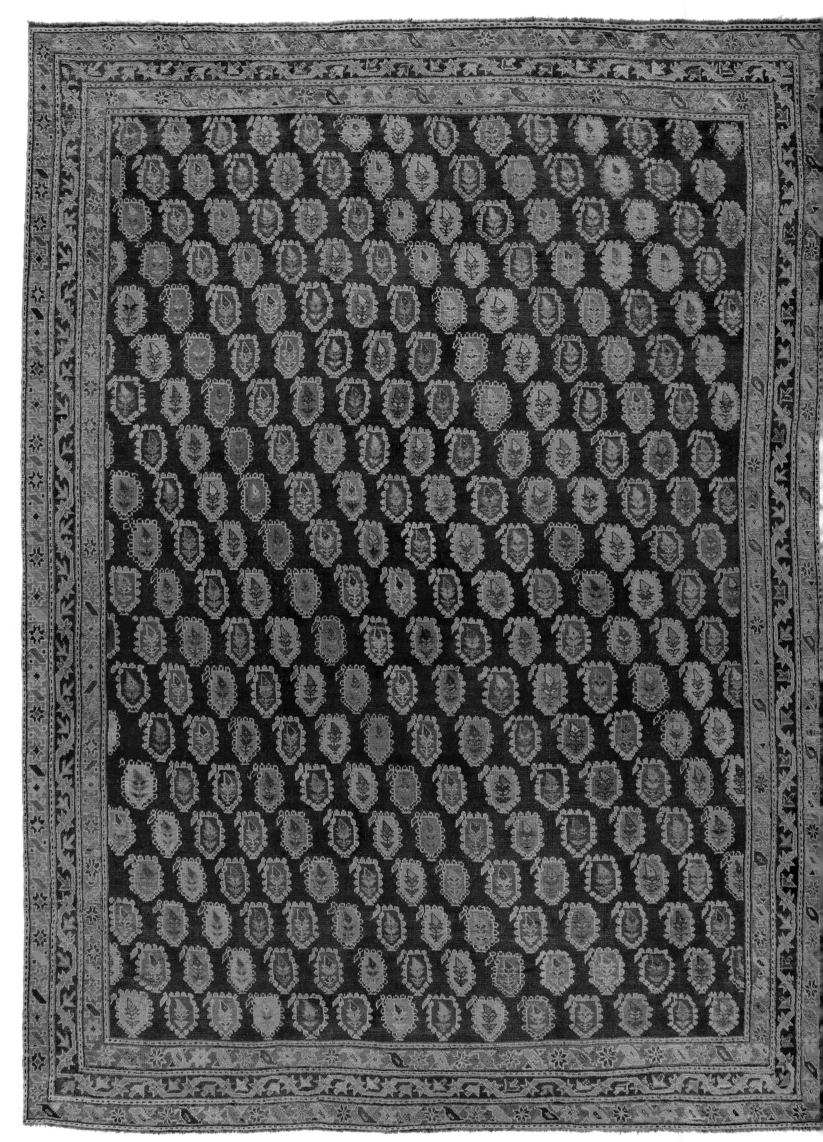

34   BB3474 Turkish Oushak 17' × 12'8″

BB4971 Turkish Oushak 24'3″ × 16'2″   35

BB4237 Chinese 14'10" × 11'10"

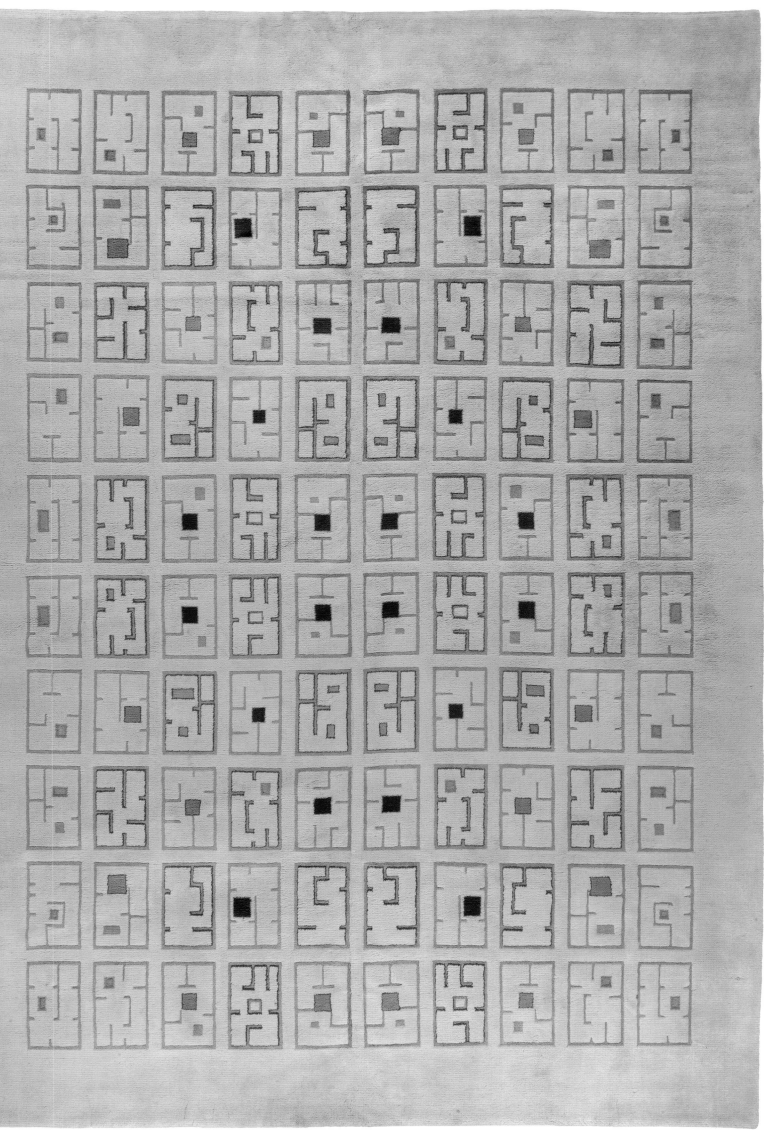

BB4970 French Rug Design by Paul Leleu 15'2″ × 11'   37

38   BB5081 Swedish Half Pile 11'10″ × 8'

BB4975 Swedish Flatweave by Sofia Widen 17'8" × 10'6"   39

40

BB5218 Chinese 11'8" × 11'5"

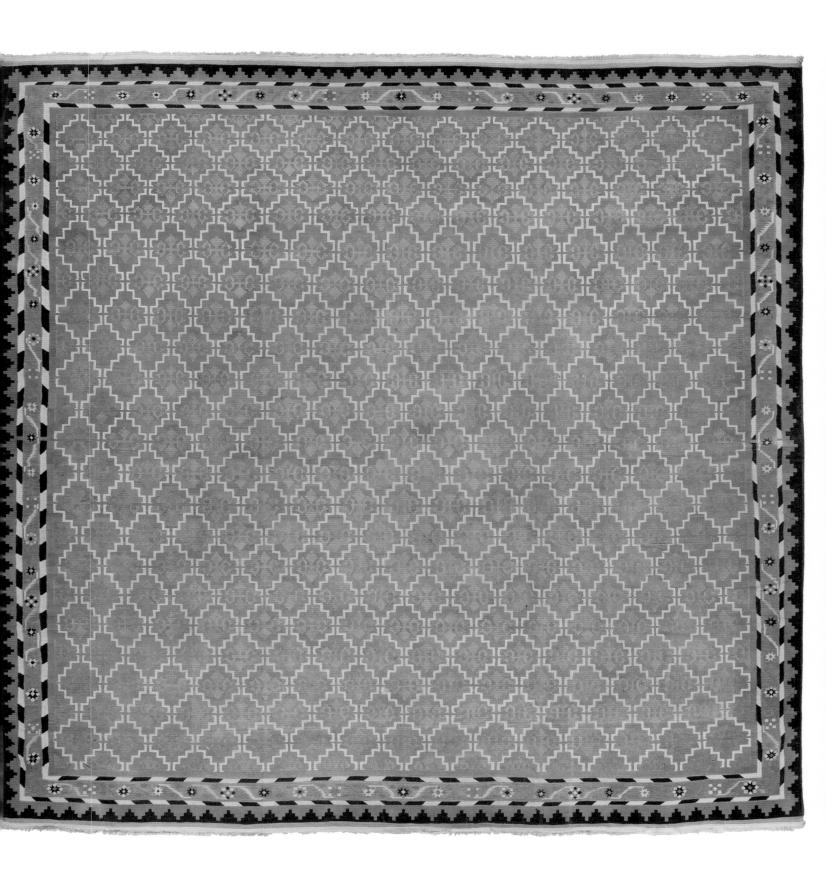

BB4824 Indian Dhurrie 14'6" × 14'6"

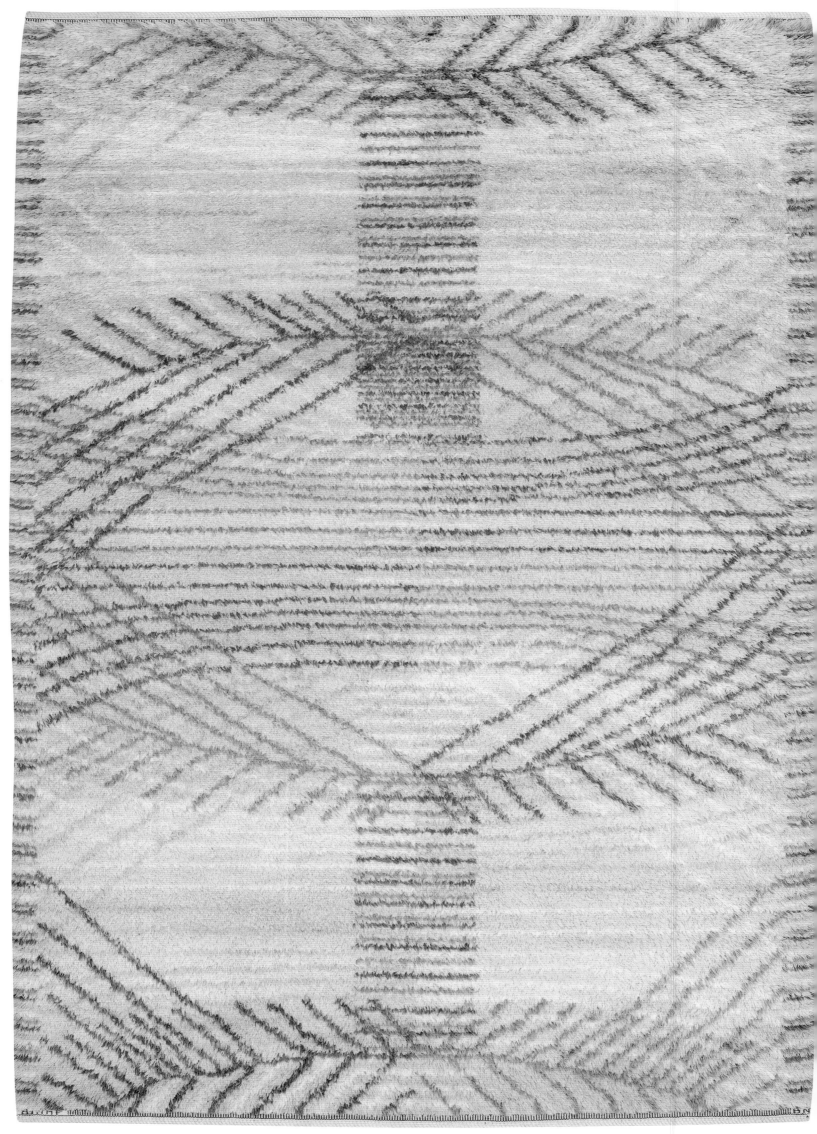

42   BB5209 Swedish Pile (Marina) by Marta Maas-Fjetterstrom 9'6" × 6'5"

3B5207 Swedish Flatweave "Orange Facade" by Marta Maas-Fjetterstrom 8'3″ × 5'7″   43

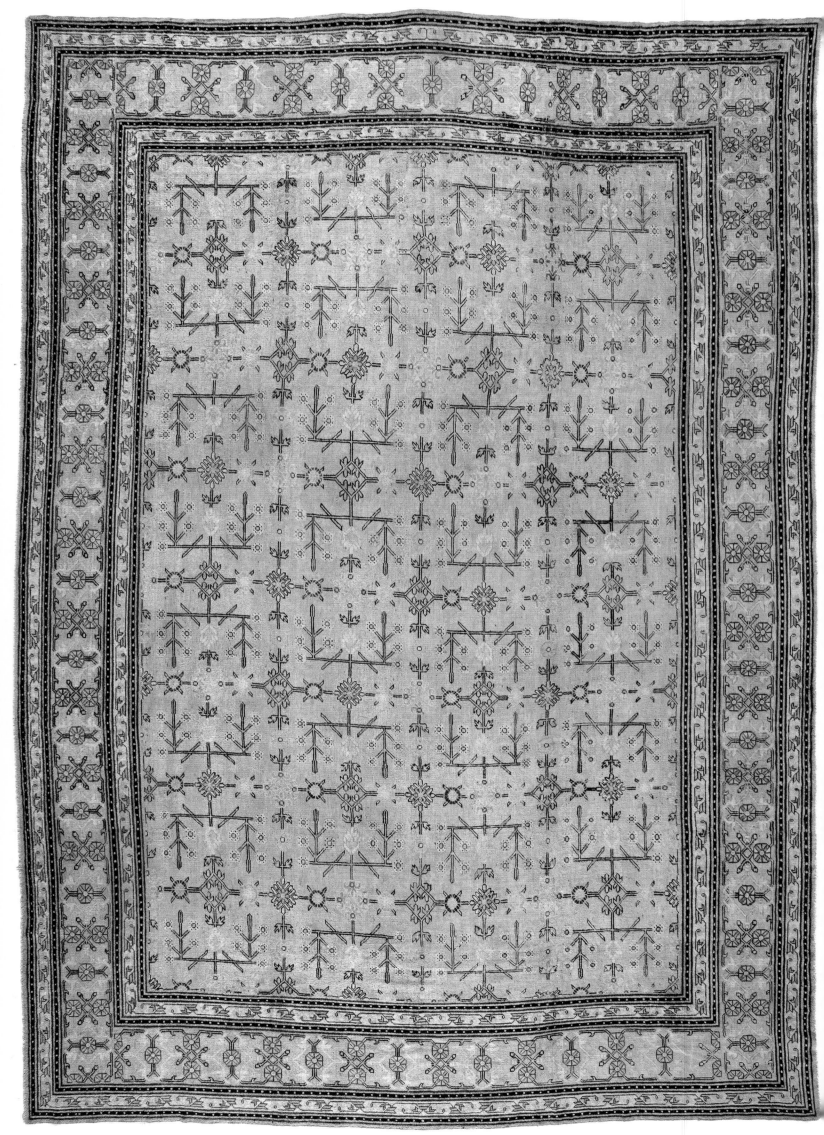

44   BB4373 Samarkand (Khotan) 17' × 13'

BB4882 Samarkand (Khotan) 14'10" × 10'6"

BB4023 Chinese Deco 13'3″ × 9'6″

BB4896 French Art Deco 20' × 14'3"

48   BB5219 French Modernist 14' × 7'2"

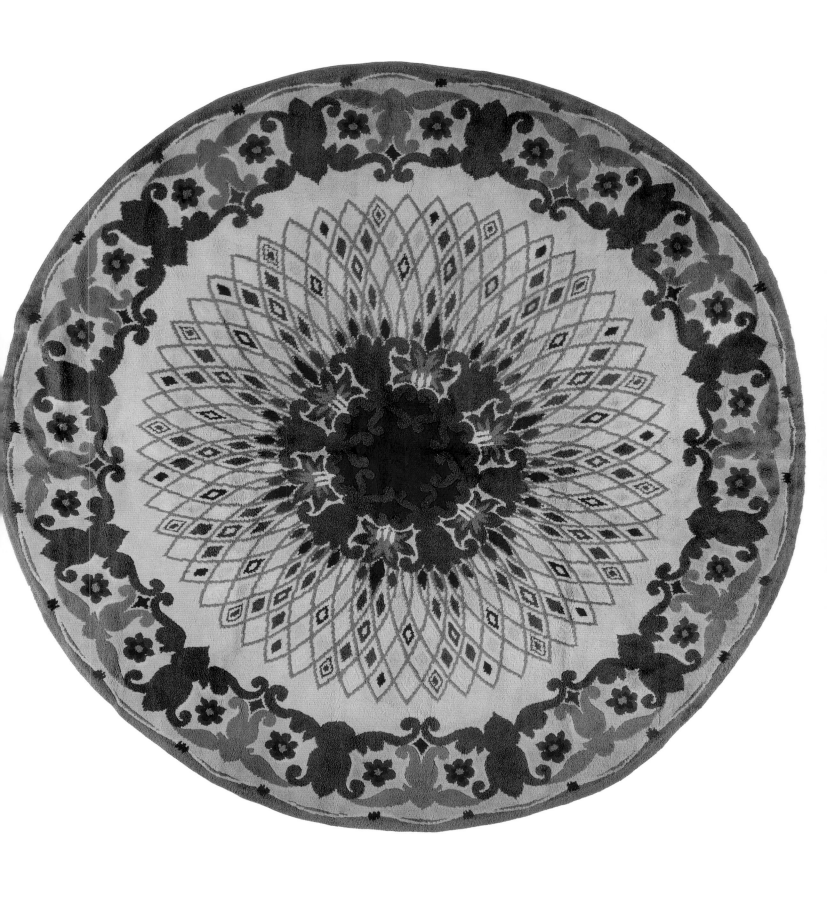

BB4792 French Deco Rug Design by Paul Leleu 10'10" × 10'9"   49

50   BB3969 Chinese Deco 15'10″ × 9'4″

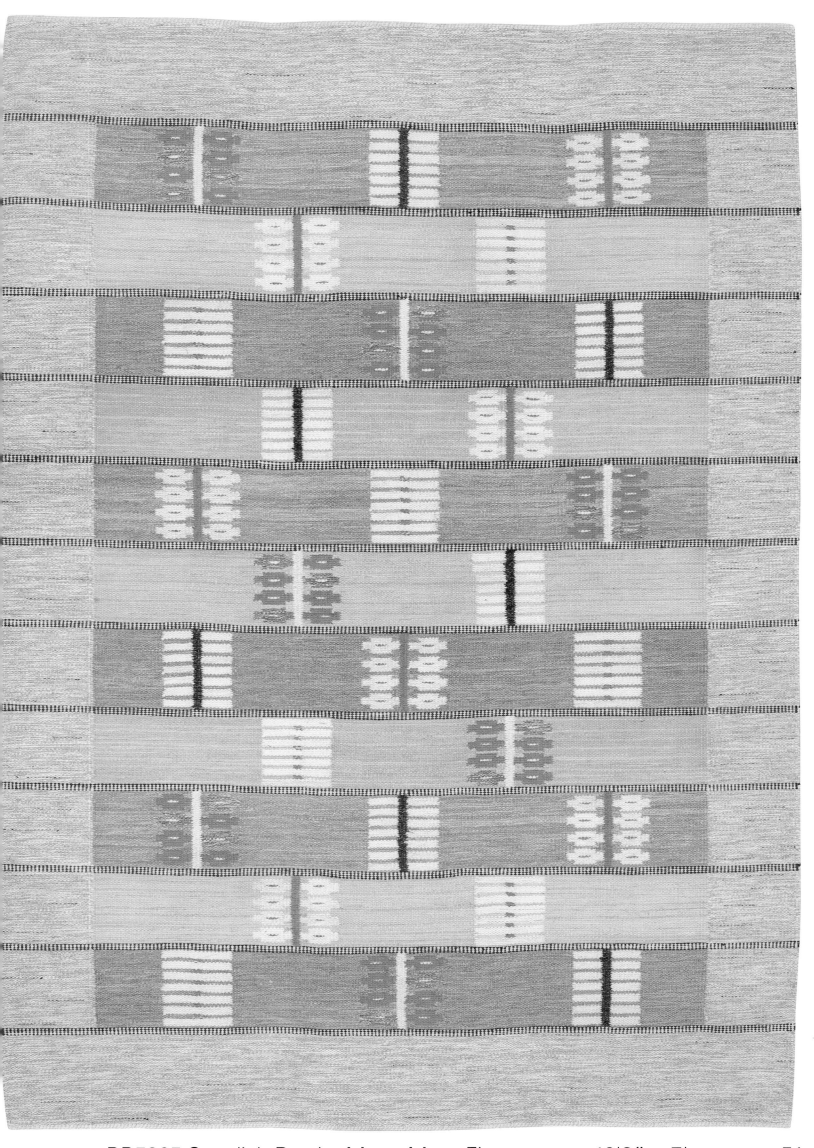

BB5205 Swedish Rug by Marta Maas-Fjetterstrom 10'3″ × 7'   51

52   BB4480 Afghan Kilim 16'9″ × 12'3″

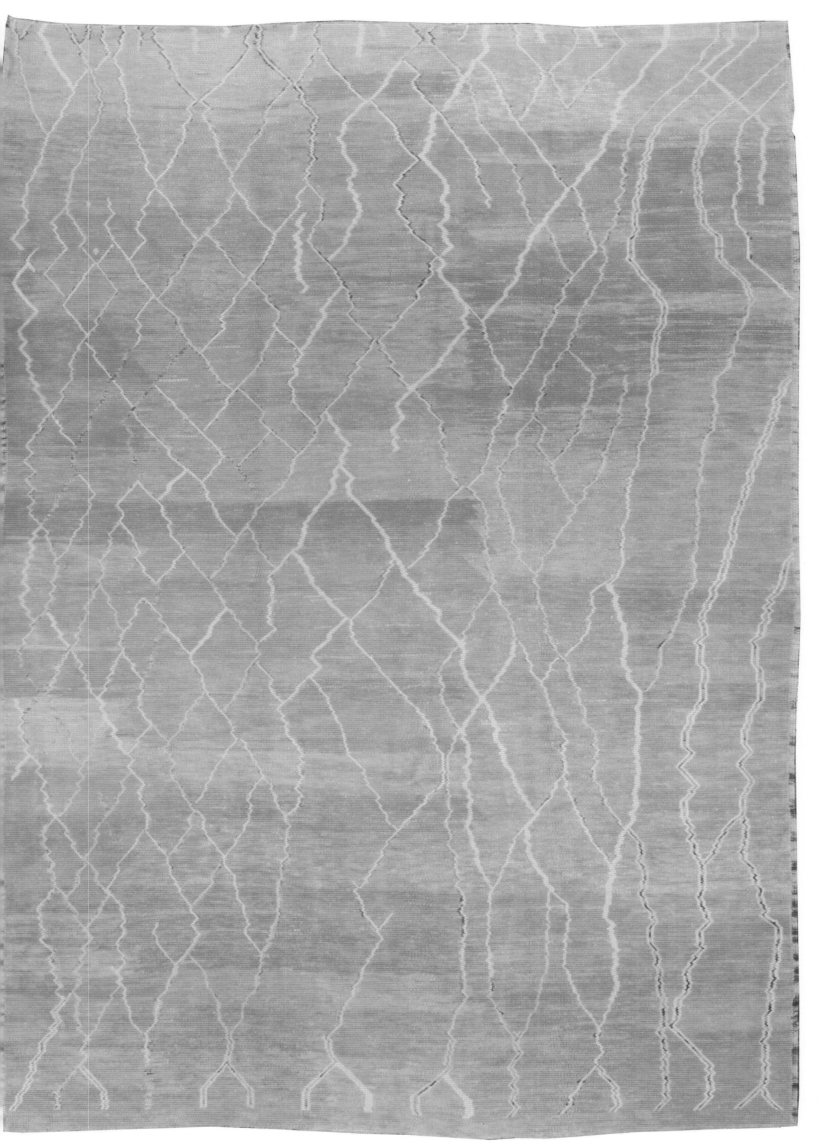

BB4483 Moroccan 11'10″ × 8'2″

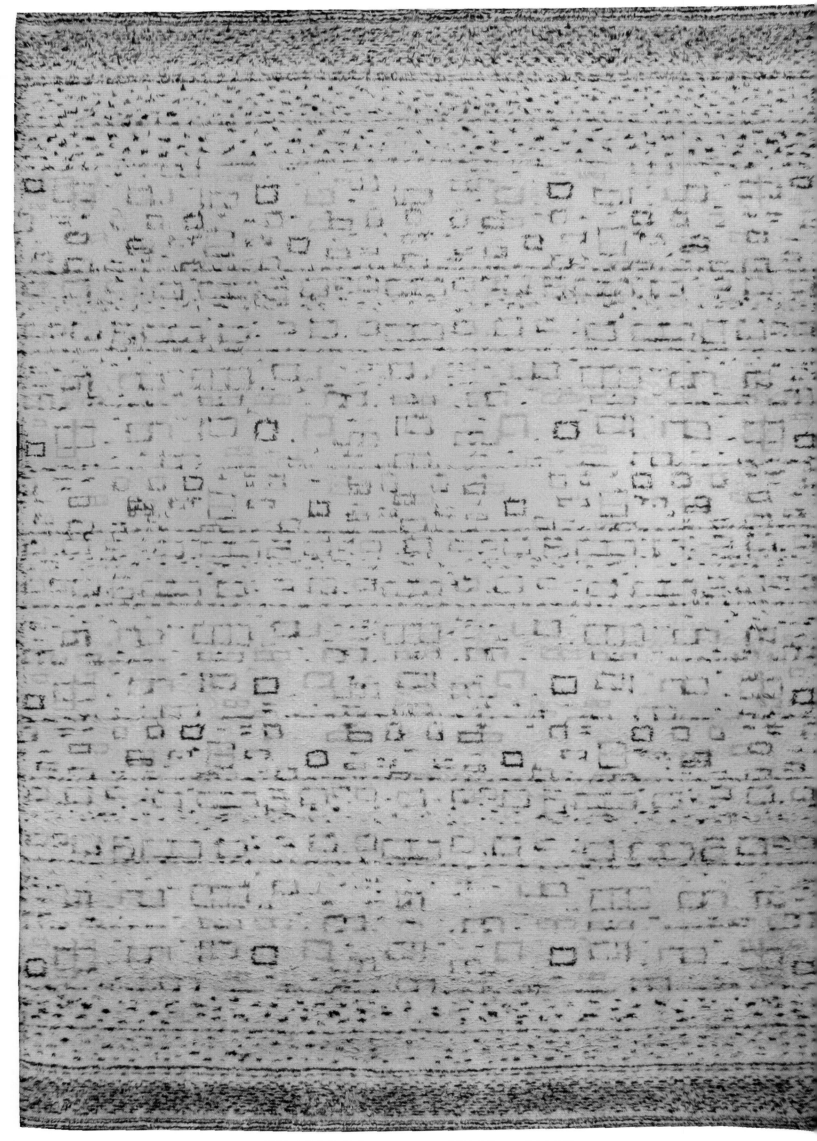

BB4690 Moroccan 13'6" × 9'10"

BB4828 Moroccan 17'6" × 7'5"

56   BB5119 Arts and Crafts Carpet by C.F.A Voysey 12'7" × 10'8"

BB5159 Arts and Crafts Carpet by C.F.A Voysey 11'4" × 8'10"　　　57

The New

At DLB we have a fascination with the past but are uniquely prepared to capture the now. Our new and custom rugs inject a space with a playful sophisticated flair, using resources all over the world to achieve a wondrous product. DLB values beauty, freshness and proportion to create our rugs. Be prepared to be dazzled by the different textures and patterns from geometric to abstract.

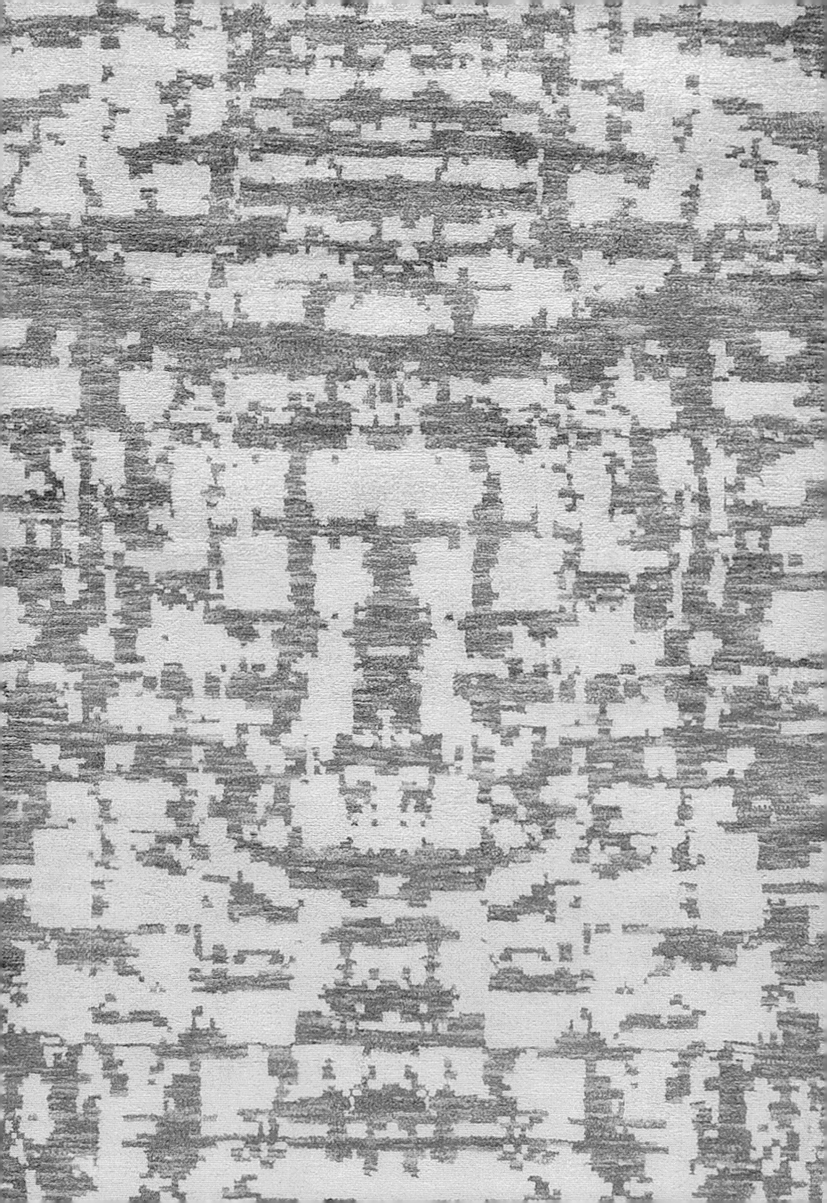

60   N10403 Kusafari by Eskayel 18' × 12'

N10301 Petra 20' × 14'

N10300 Crocodile 23'5″ × 15'

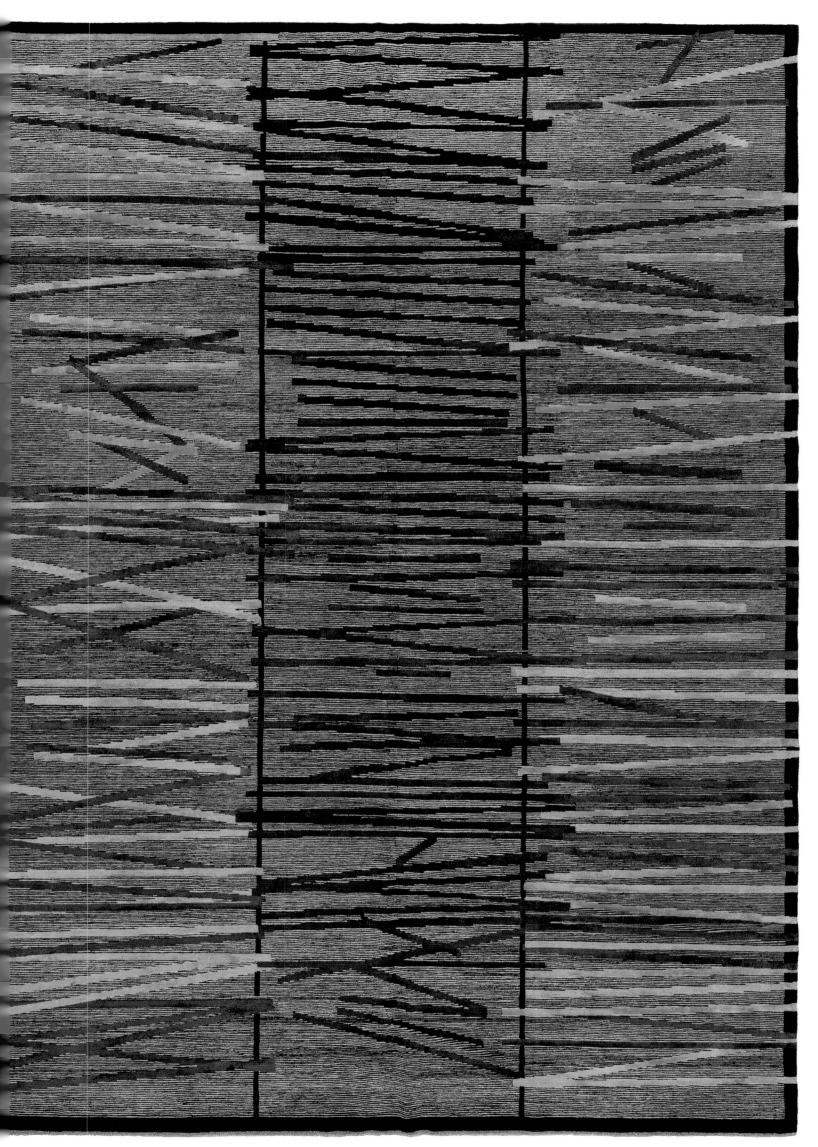

N10396 Dover 12'3″ × 9'4″

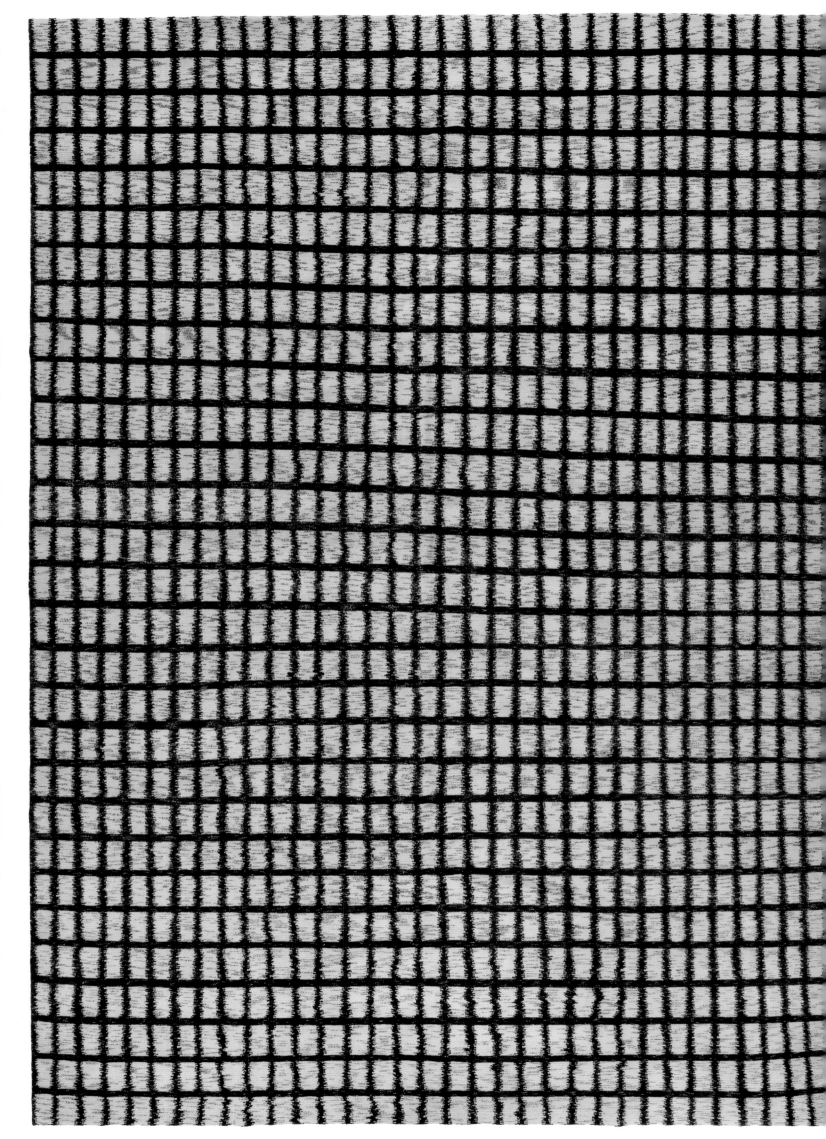

N10359 White Magic 13'10″ × 9'10″

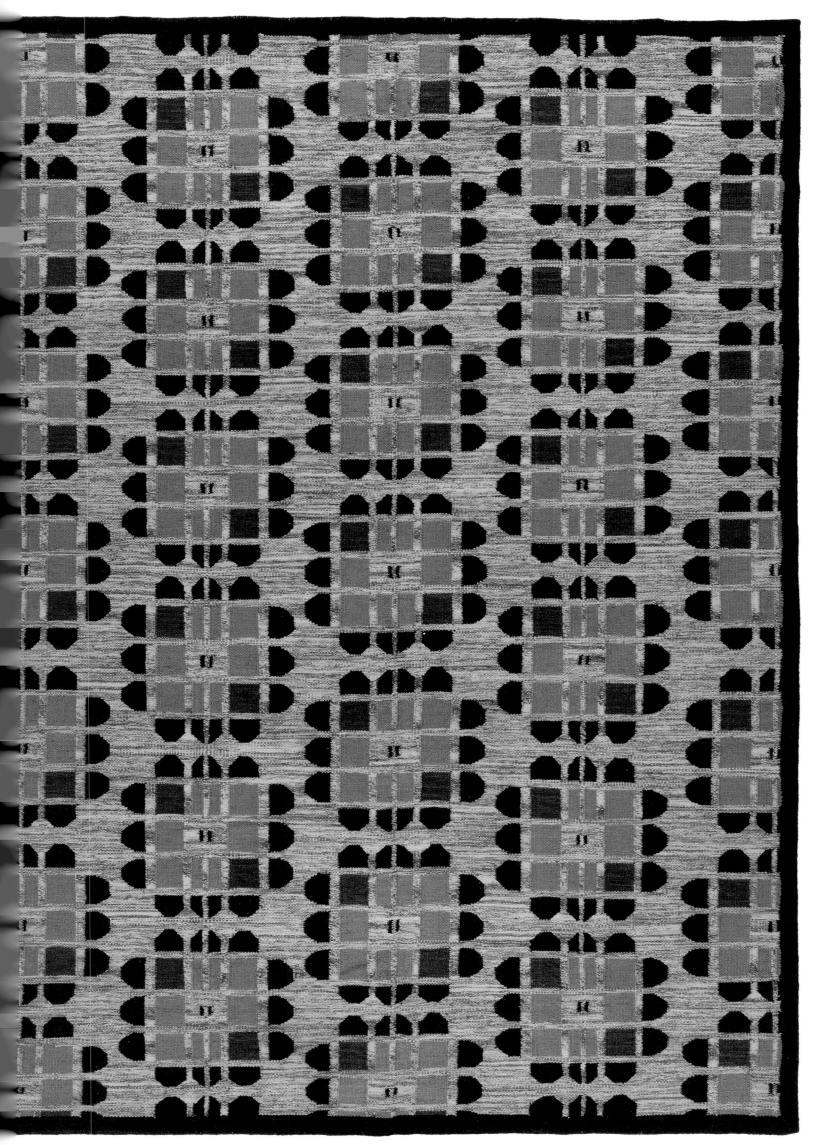

N10341 Dahillas 12'3″ × 9'

N10219 Hemp Modern 20'6″ × 14'

N10381 Vittono 15' × 12'

N10336 Alhambra 14'3" × 10'3"

N10361 Cuenca 9'2" × 5'6"

N10303 Sun Flower 12' × 9'

N10404 Green Evolution 15' × 10'

N10354 Caramel Grids 14' × 10'

N10402 Silk Vases 10' × 8'

74   4ab01 Blue Pomegranate 14'2" × 10'

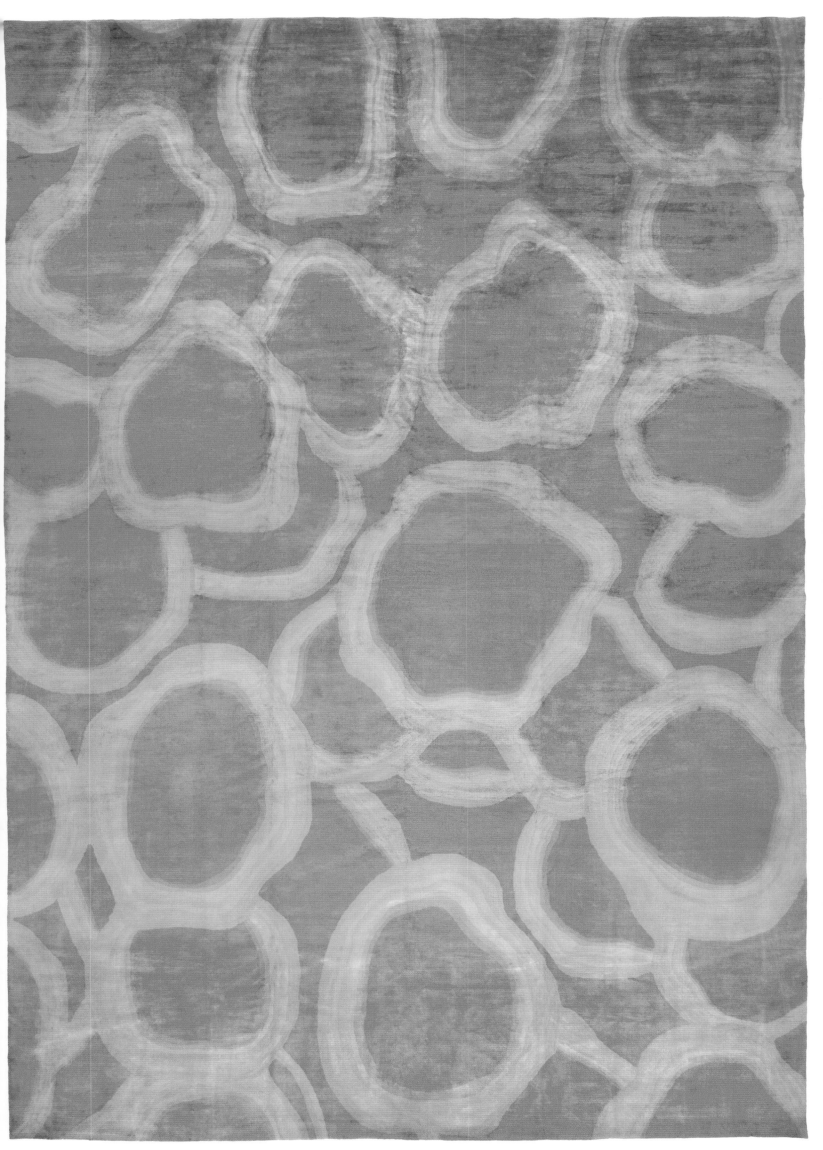

N1030 Ondulation 22'10″ × 14'

76   N10017 Ottoman 14' × 10'

N10273 Desau Flatweave 20' × 15'

N1004 Symmetry 14' × 10'

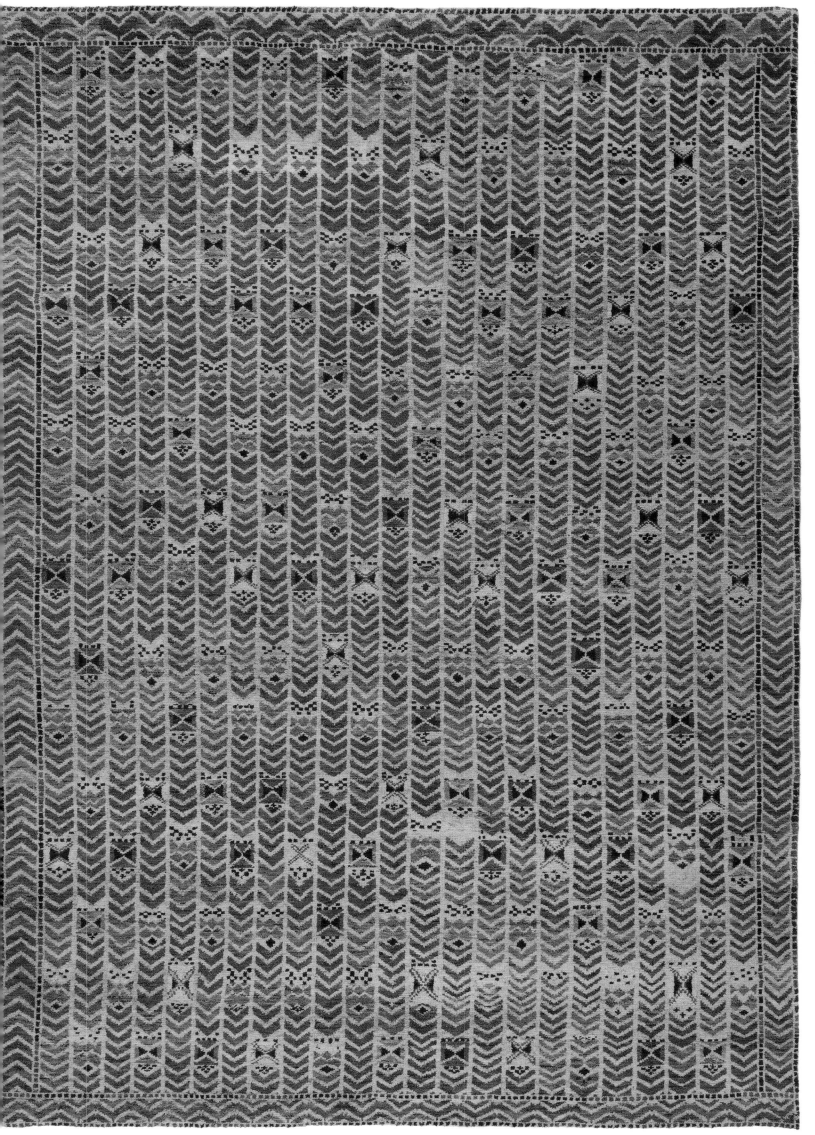

N10401 Marta 12' × 8'8″

N10339 Ripple Pearl by Eskayel 14'3″ × 10'2″

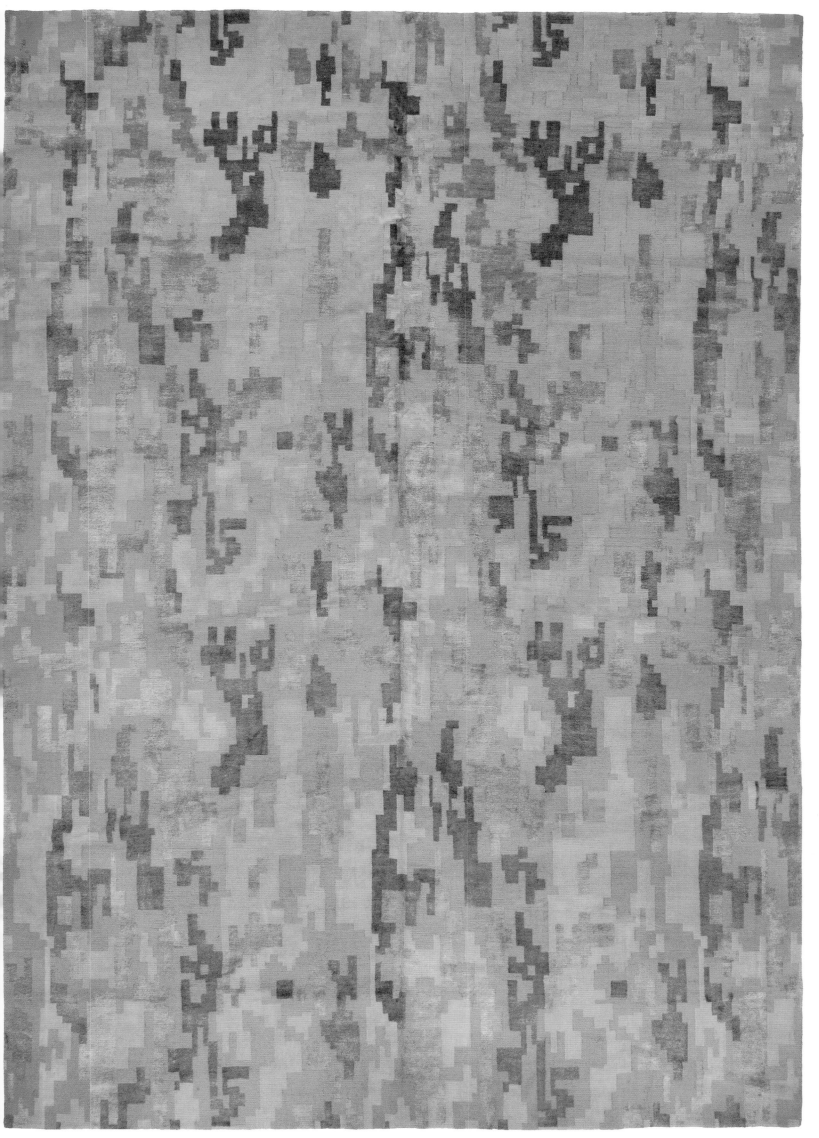

N10204 Arthur Dunnam 17'3" ×12'7"

N10400 Moroccan 11'2″ ×11'7″

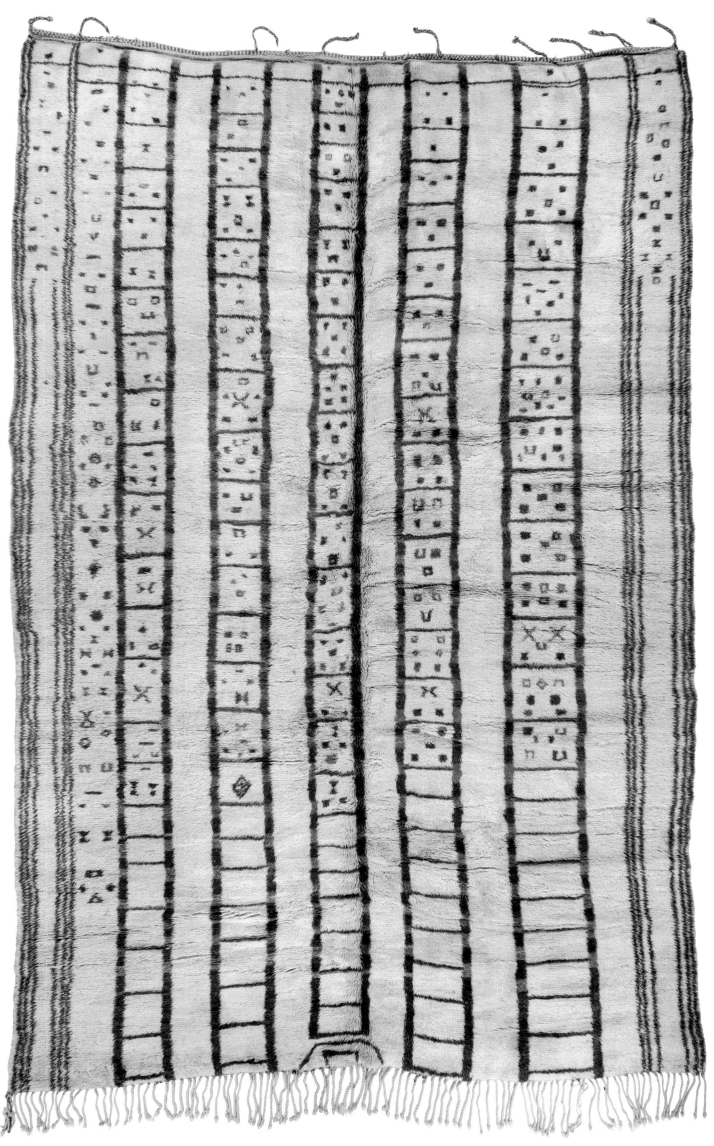

N10214 Moroccan 15'8″ × 10'3″ 83

N10012 Samarkand 17'2″ × 13'5″

N10265 Anatolia 11'6″ × 8'5″

N10372 Blossom 12' × 8'10″

The Future!

Stay tuned we have just begun…

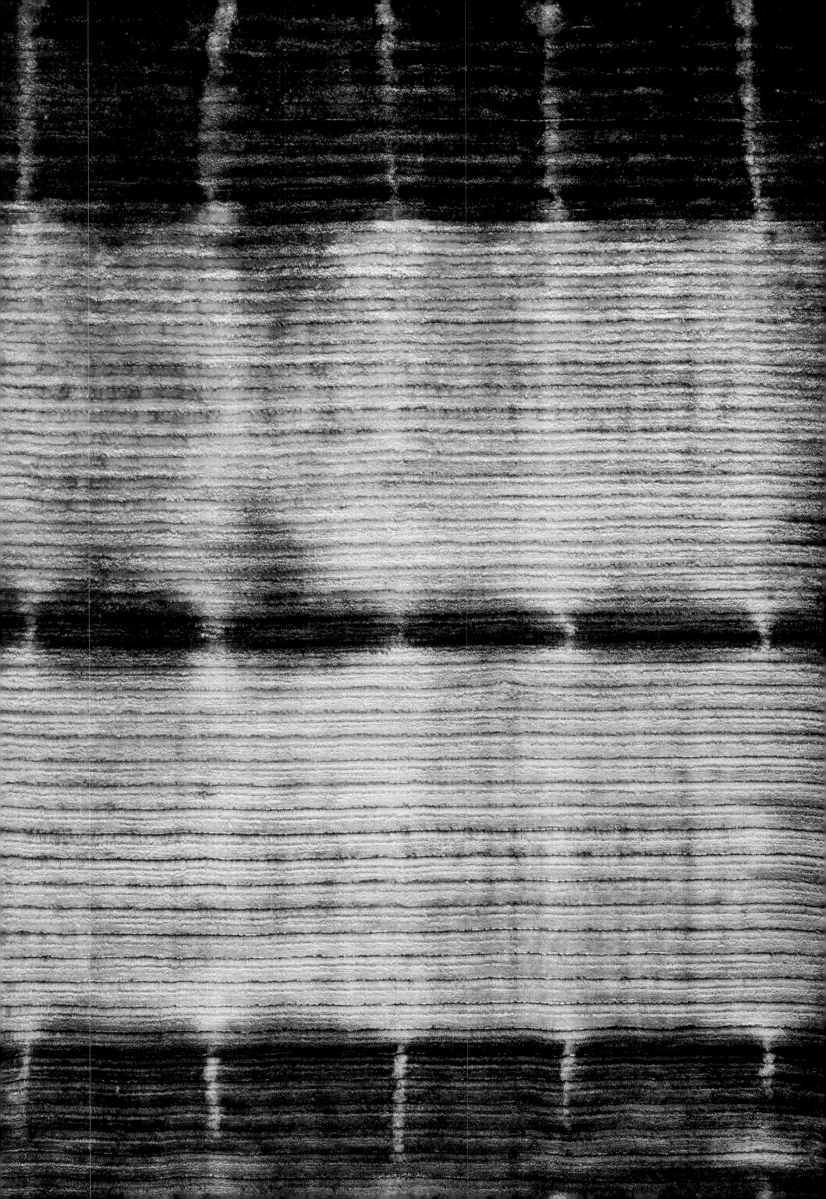

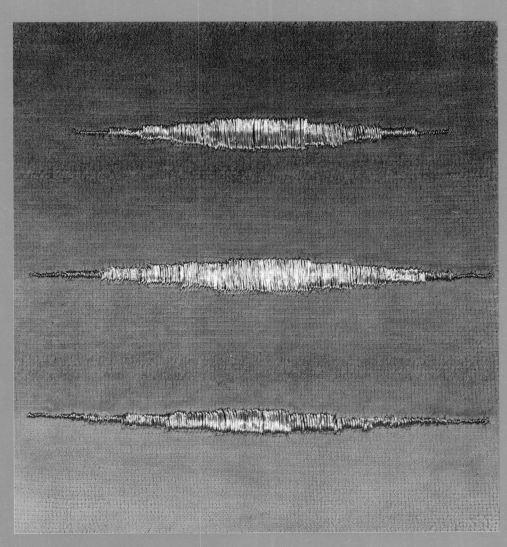

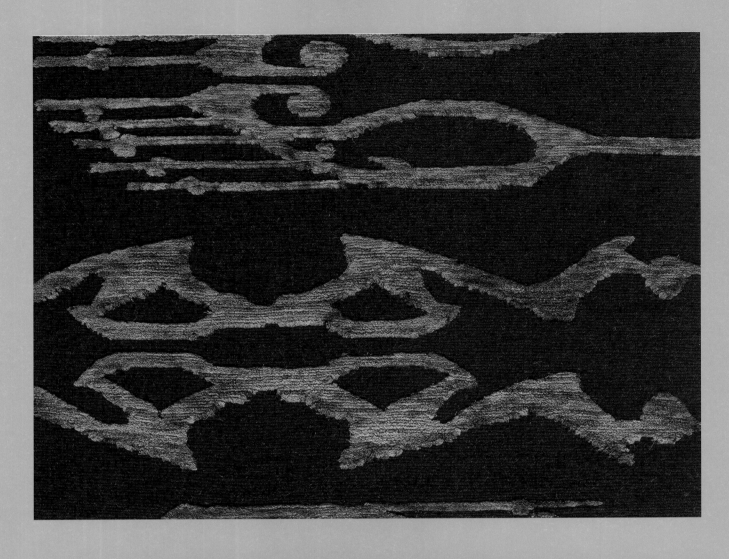

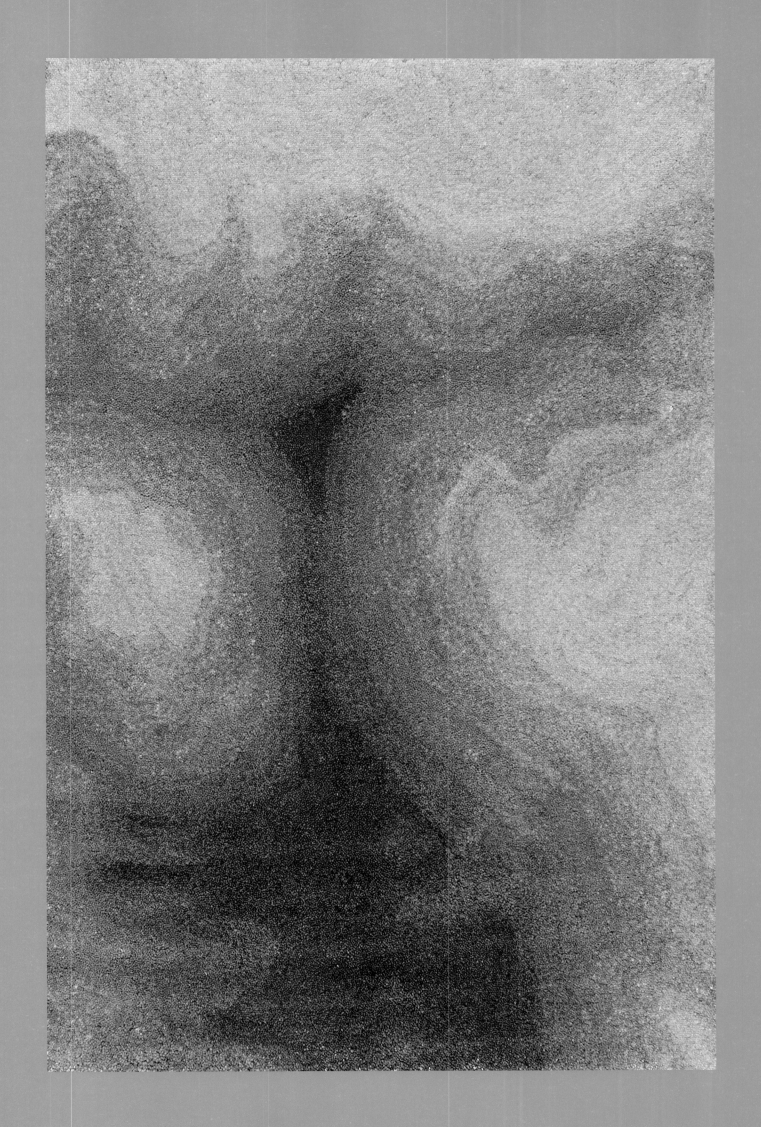

95

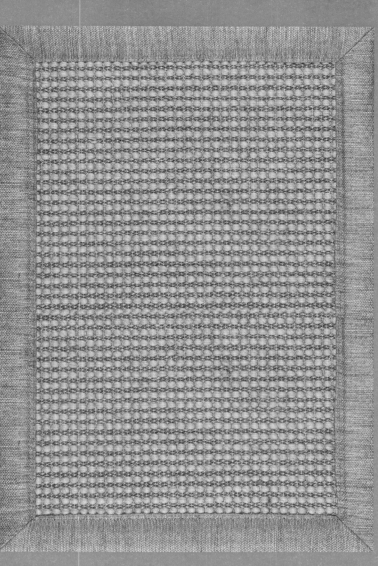

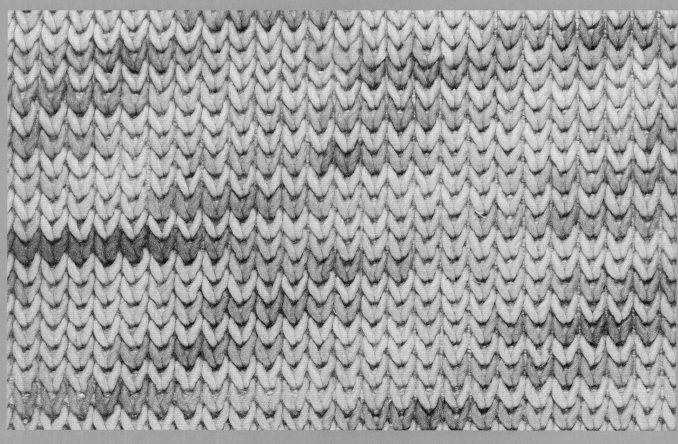

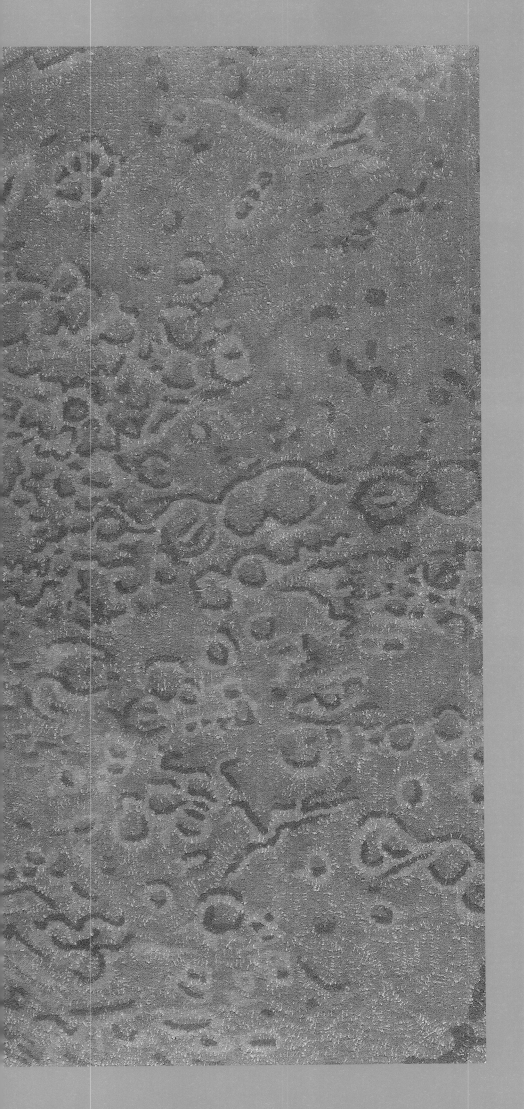
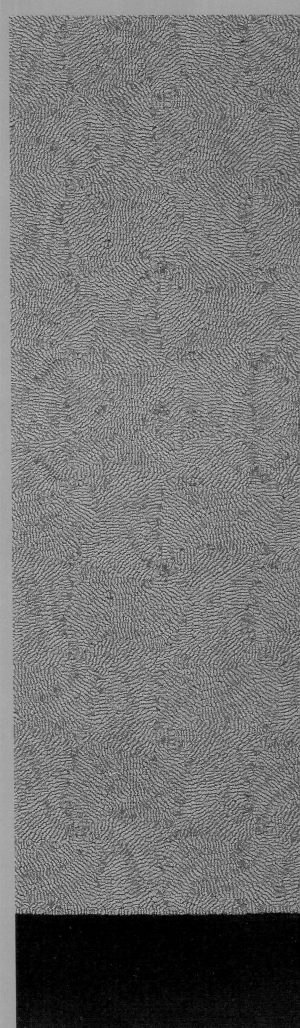

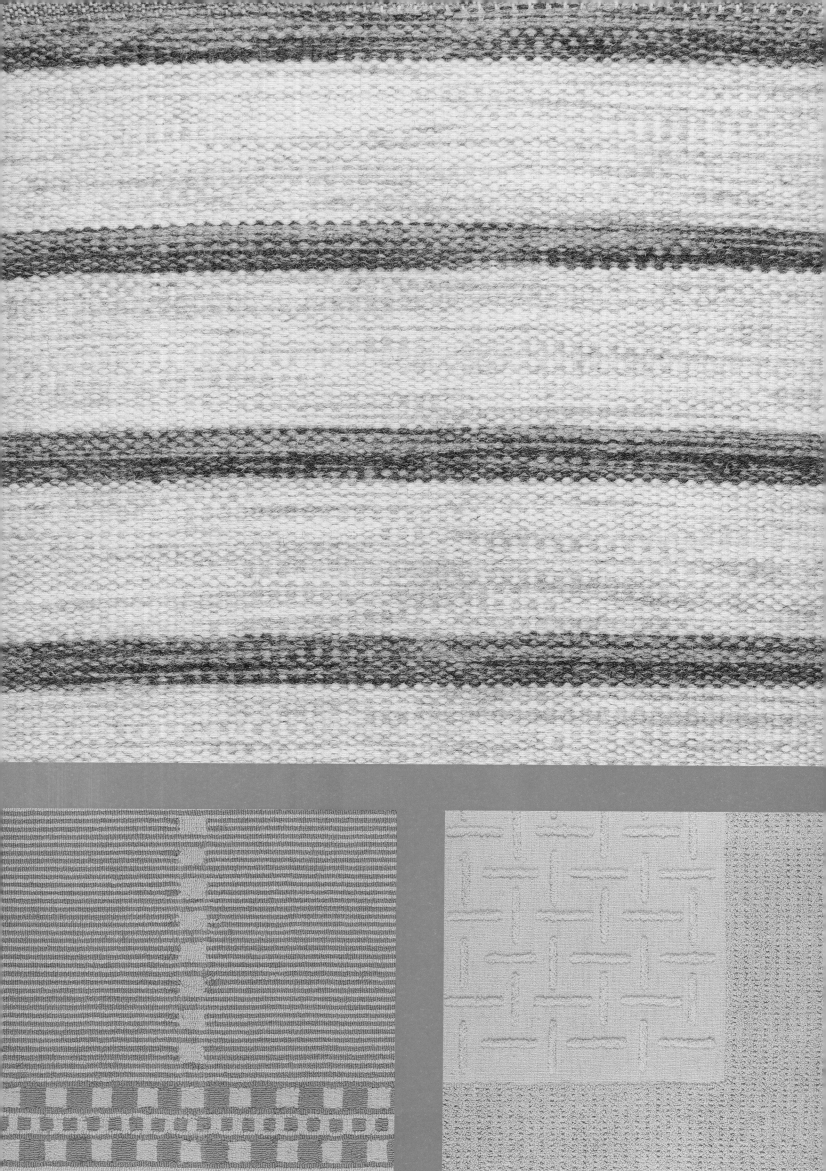

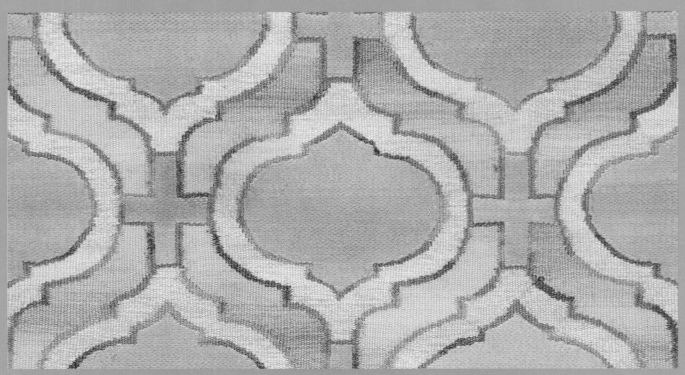

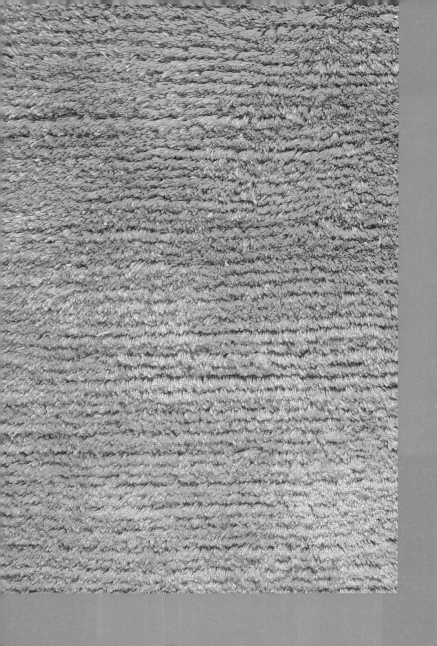

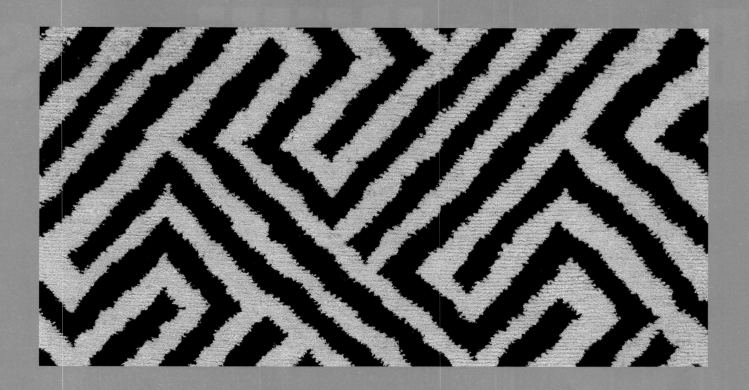

Bunny Williams

World renowned designer Bunny Williams is proud to announce her rug collection with Doris Leslie Blau. The collection is comprised of all-over patterns that are stylized versions of classic motifs. Colors range from tone-on-tone neutrals and muted blues and greens to rich blues reminiscent of the Aegean Sea. Offered in hemp pile, cut pile, silk/wool blends, aloe/wool blends, looped pile and flat weaves the collection is as eclectic and expressive as Williams' design work. "Rugs are the magic of every room," says Williams. "For me, they are where I begin every project. I choose a beautiful rug then select paint colors and fabrics that complement it. For years I have come to Doris Leslie Blau because I know they have rugs, both old and new, that a designer can really build a room around. When I began working on my own rug collection, there was no hesitation in my choice to collaborate with Nader and Doris Leslie Blau."

Bunny Williams was raised in Charlottesville, VA and lives in New York City, Connecticut, and the Dominican Republic with her husband, antiques dealer John Rosselli, and their beloved dogs. She started Bunny Williams Inc. in 1988 after working with the legendary design firm Parish-Hadley Associates for 22 years, and prior to that the prestigious antique firm Stair & Co. Today she not only runs her design firm, but with her husband John Rosselli, owns Treillage Ltd., two shops selling garden objects, antiques, and decorative accessories, based in New York. In 2008 she introduced a celebrated home furnishings collection, Bunny Williams Home, which continues to expand and introduce new pieces. Williams' fourth book, "Scrapbook for Living" was published by Stewart, Tabori & Chang in November 2010.

Bunny Williams

HOME

To view Bunny Williams' full collection of rugs please visit:
www.DorisLeslieBlau.com/bunny-williams

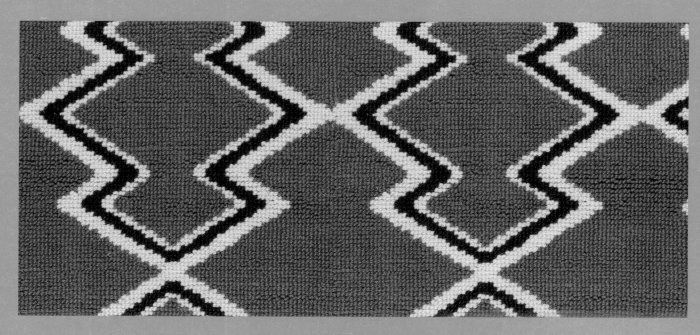

Aztec

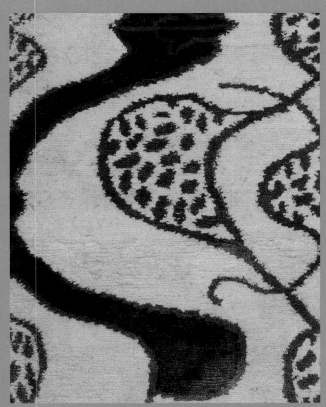

Taj

Aegean

Sundance Stripe

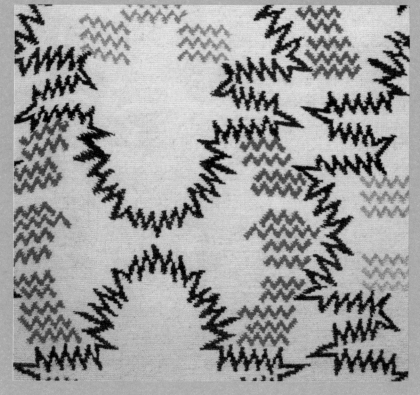

Paleo

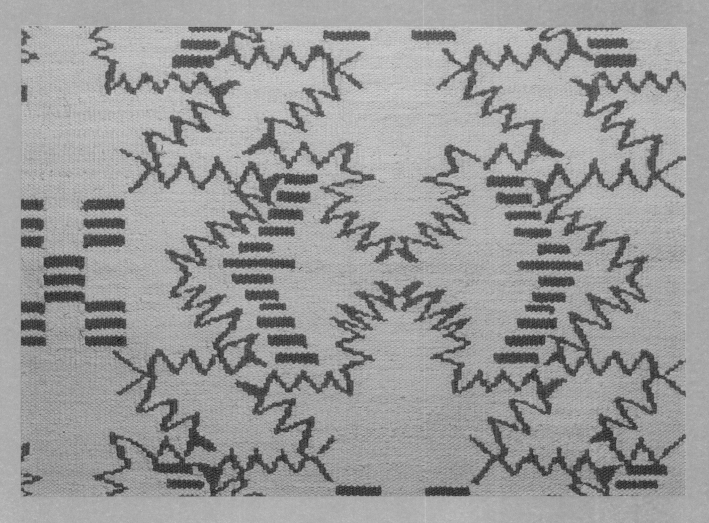

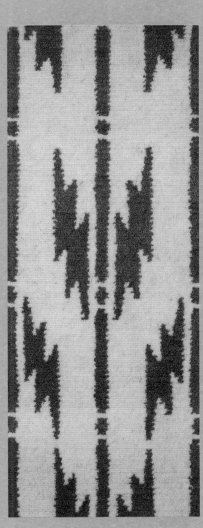

Green Paleo

Quiver

Index

Art Director: Nader Bolour

Editor: Dorian Bernstein

Photographer: Farshad Namdar

MAIN SHOWROOM   306 E. 61st Street, 7th Floor, New York, NY 10065

D&D BUILDING   979 3rd Avenue, Suite 625, New York, NY 10022

Tel. 212-586-5511   Email: nader@dorisleslieblau.com

www.dorisleslieblau.com